STUDY GUIDE

Bearstone
Will Hobbs

WITH CONNECTIONS

HOLT, RINEHART AND WINSTON
Harcourt Brace & Company
Austin • New York • Orlando • Atlanta • San Francisco • Boston • Dallas • Toronto • London

Staff Credits

Associate Director: Mescal Evler

Manager of Editorial Operations: Robert R. Hoyt

Managing Editor: Bill Wahlgren

Executive Editor: Emily Shenk

Editor: Cheryl Christian

Editorial Staff: *Assistant Managing Editor,* Mandy Beard; *Copyediting Supervisor,* Michael Neibergall; *Senior Copyeditor,* Mary Malone; *Copyeditors,* Joel Bourgeois, Jon Hall, Jeffrey T. Holt, Jane M. Kominek, Susan Sandoval; *Editorial Coordinators,* Marie H. Price, Jill Chertudi, Mark Holland, Marcus Johnson, Tracy DeMont; *Support Staff,* Pat Stover, Matthew Villalobos; *Word Processors,* Ruth Hooker, Margaret Sanchez, Kelly Keeley

Permissions: Carrie Jones, Catherine Paré

Design: *Art Director, Book & Media Design,* Joe Melomo

Image Services: *Art Buyer, Supervisor,* Elaine Tate

Prepress Production: Beth Prevelige, Sergio Durante

Manufacturing Coordinator: Michael Roche

Development Coordinator: Diane B. Engel

Copyright © by Holt, Rinehart and Winston

All rights reserved. No part of this publication may be reproduced or transmitted in any form or by any means, electronic or mechanical, including photocopy, recording, or any information storage and retrieval system, without permission in writing from the publisher.

Teachers using HRW LIBRARY may photocopy blackline masters in complete pages in sufficient quantities for classroom use only and not for resale.

Cover Illustration: Higgens Bond/ American Artist Rep., Inc.

HRW is a registered trademark licensed to Holt, Rinehart and Winston.

Printed in the United States of America

ISBN 0-03-054034-8

123456 085 02 01 00 99 98

TABLE of CONTENTS

FOR THE TEACHER

Using This Study Guide 2

Tips for Classroom Management 3

Strategies for Inclusion 4

Assessment Options 5

About the Writer 6

About the Novel 7

Key Elements: Plot / Theme / Characters / Setting / Point of View / Figures of Speech / Foreshadowing 8–12

Resources Overview .... inside front cover	Answer Key 45–52

FOR THE STUDENT

Before You Read: Activities 13

Chapters 1–8: Making Meanings / Choices 14–15

Chapters 9–15: Making Meanings / Choices 16–17

Chapters 16–22: Making Meanings / Choices 18–19

Novel Projects: Cross-Curricular Connections / Multimedia and Internet Connections 20–21

Exploring the Connections: Making Meanings 22–24

    Denning with the Great Bear, by Will Hobbs 22

    the earth is a living thing, by Lucille Clifton 22

    Baby Bear Moon, by Joseph Bruchac and Jonathan London 22

    Here on This Mountain, by Nancy Wood 22

    Dancer, by Vickie Sears 23

    Lesson 1 and Lesson 2, by Pat Mora 23

    My Friend Flicka, by Mary O'Hara 24

    The Name Game, from A Book About Names, by Milton Meltzer 24

Novel Notes: Issues 1–6 25–30

Reading Skills and Strategies Worksheets: Novel Organizer / Charting Causes and Effects /
    Completing a Story Triangle / Using a Time line 31–35

Literary Elements Worksheets: Figures of Speech / Foreshadowing 36–37

Glossary 38

Vocabulary Worksheet 39

Test 40–43

Using This Study Guide

This Study Guide is intended to
- *help students become active and engaged readers*
- *deepen students' enjoyment and understanding of literature*
- *provide you with multiple options for guiding students through the novel and the Connections and for evaluating students' progress*

Most of the pages in this Study Guide are reproducible so that you can, if you choose, give students the opportunity to work independently.

Key Elements
- plot summary and analysis
- major themes
- character summaries
- notes on setting, point of view, and other literary elements

Making Meanings
- First Thoughts
- Shaping Interpretations
- Connecting with the Text
- Extending the Text
- Challenging the Text

A **Reading Check** focuses on review and comprehension.

The Worksheets
- **Reading Skills and Strategies Worksheets** focus on reading and critical-thinking strategies and skills.
- **Literary Elements Worksheets** guide students in considering and analyzing literary elements (discussed in **Key Elements**) important to understanding the novel.
- **Vocabulary Worksheets** provide practice with Vocabulary Words. Activities target synonyms, affixes, roots, context clues, and other vocabulary elements.

For the Teacher

About the Writer Biographical highlights supplement the author biography that appears in the HRW Library edition of this novel. Sidebars list works by and about the writer as resources for teaching and for students' research.

About the Novel A critical history summarizes responses to the novel, including excerpts from reviews. Sidebars suggest audiovisual and multimedia resources.

Key Elements Significant literary elements of the novel are introduced. These elements recur in the questions, activities, worksheets, and assessment tools.

For the Student: reproducible masters

Before You Read: Activities *(preparation for beginning the novel)* Motivating activities lead students to explore ideas and topics they will encounter in the novel.

Making Meanings *(for each section of the novel)* Questions move students from immediate personal response to high-level critical thinking.

Choices: Building Your Portfolio *(for each section of the novel)* The activities suggested here involve students in exploring different aspects of the novel on their own or collaboratively. The results may be included in a portfolio, developed further, or used as springboards for larger projects.

Novel Projects *(culminating activities)* Cross-Curricular, Multimedia, and Internet projects relate to the novel as a whole. Project ideas can be adapted for individual, pair, or group presentations.

Exploring the Connections *(a set of Making Meanings questions for each of the Connections readings)* Questions encourage students to relate the readings to the themes and topics of the novel.

Novel Notes *(multiple issues)* These one-page news sheets provide high-interest background information relating to historical, cultural, literary, and other elements of the novel. They are intended for distribution *after* students have begun the novel section the issue supplements.

Reading Skills and Strategies Worksheets *(one for each section of the novel, plus a Novel Organizer)*

Literary Elements Worksheets *(end of novel)*

Vocabulary Worksheets *(during or after reading)*

Glossary, with Vocabulary Words *(to use throughout the novel)* This list of words from the novel serves as a mini-dictionary that students may refer to as they read. **Highlighted Vocabulary Words** support vocabulary acquisition.

Test *(end of novel)* A mix of objective and short-answer questions covering the whole novel provides a traditional form of assessment. Essay questions consist of five optional writing prompts.

Tips for Classroom Management

Preparing Students for Reading
Set aside a time each week for talking about books. On the right are some ideas for introducing a novel and motivating students to pick it up and begin reading.

Reading and Responding
Book groups Although most students will read independently, discussions with classmates can enrich their reading enormously. This Study Guide suggests appropriate points to stop and talk about the story so far. At these stopping points, the **Making Meanings** questions can be used as discussion starters. Ask groups to keep a simple log of their discussions.

Full-class discussions Engage students by beginning the discussion with a question that encourages a personal response (see **First Thoughts** in **Making Meanings**). As students respond to the questions involving interpretation, invite them to support their inferences and conclusions with evidence from the text. Encourage a noncritical environment. Show your own enthusiasm for the novel—it's infectious!

Reader's logs Logs, journals, and notebooks offer an open and nonthreatening yet systematic mode for students to respond in writing to the novel. Making entries as they read can help students learn more about themselves as readers, monitor their own progress, and write more easily and fluently. Keeping logs can also enhance participation in small-group and class discussions of the novel. Consider dialogue journals in which two readers—a student and you, a classmate, or a family member—exchange thoughts about their reading. **Reader's Log** suggestions appear in each issue of **Novel Notes**.

Cooperative learning Small groups may meet both to discuss the novel and to plan and work on projects related to the novel (see ideas in **Choices** and in **Novel Projects**). Encourage full participation by making sure that each group member has a defined role and that the roles rotate so that the same student is not always the leader or the recorder, for example.

Projects While students' projects can extend into other content areas, they should always contribute to enriching and extending students' understanding of the novel itself. If students know when they begin the novel that presenting a project will be a part of their evaluation, they can begin early to brainstorm, discuss, and try out ideas. Project ideas can come from **Novel Notes**, from the **Choices** activities, from the **Novel Projects** ideas, and, of course, from the students themselves. Projects can be developed and presented by individuals, pairs, or groups.

Reflecting
When students finish the novel, they should not be left with a test as the culminating experience. Project presentations can be a kind of celebration, as can a concluding discussion. On the right are some ideas for a reflective discussion. They can be used in a whole-class environment, or small groups can choose certain questions to answer and share their conclusions (or their disagreements) with the class.

Ideas for Introducing the Novel
- Give a brief book talk to arouse students' curiosity and interest (see **About the Novel** for ideas).
- Play or show a segment of an audio, film, or video version of the book or an interview with the writer.
- Present high-interest biographical information about the writer (see **About the Writer** in this Study Guide and the biographical sketch at the end of the HRW Library edition of this novel).
- Read aloud a passage from the novel that arouses your own interest, and elicit predictions, inferences, and speculations from students.
- Lead a focused class discussion or suggest activities that (1) draw on students' prior knowledge or (2) lead them to generate their own ideas about a significant topic or theme they will encounter in the novel (see **Before You Read**).

Reader's Log Starters
- When I began reading this book, I thought…
- My favorite part, so far, is…
- I predict that…
- I like the way the writer…
- I'd like to ask the writer…
- If I had written this book, I would have…
- This [character, incident, idea] reminds me of…
- This book made me think about…
- This book made me realize…

Questions for Reflection
- What was your favorite part of the book (and why)?
- If you could be one of the characters, who would it be (and why)?
- Would you or wouldn't you recommend this book to a friend (and why)?
- What is the most important thing about this book?
- Would you change the ending? If not, what makes it work? If yes, what changes would you make?
- If you could have a conversation with the writer, what would you say or ask?

Study Guide | 3

Strategies for Inclusion

Each set of activities has been developed to meet special student interests, abilities, and learning styles. Because the questions and activities in this Study Guide are directed to the students, there are no labels to indicate the types of learners they target. However, in each Before You Read, Choices, and Novel Projects page, you will find activities to meet the needs of

- *less proficient readers*
- *students acquiring English*
- *advanced students*

The activities and projects have been prepared to accommodate these different learning styles:

- *auditory/musical*
- *interpersonal*
- *intrapersonal*
- *kinesthetic*
- *logical/mathematical*
- *verbal/linguistic*
- *visual/spatial*

Using the Study Guide Questions and Activities

Encourage students to adapt the suggestions given in the Study Guide to fit their own learning styles and interests. It is important to remember that students are full of surprises, and a question or activity that is challenging to an advanced student can also be handled successfully by students who are less proficient readers. The high interest level, flexibility, and variety of these questions and activities make them appropriate for a range of students.

Students should be encouraged to vary the types of activities they choose so that the same student is not regularly selecting writing or researching activities over those involving speaking, art, and performing, and vice versa. Individual and group work should also alternate, so that students have the opportunity to work on their own and as part of collaborative learning groups.

Working in Pairs and Groups

When students with varying abilities, cultural backgrounds, and learning styles work together, they can arrive at a deeper understanding of both the novel and one another.

Reading pairs can stop and check each other's responses to the novel at frequent intervals.

Students from different cultural groups can interview one another about how certain situations, character interactions, character motivations, and so on would be viewed in their home cultures.

Visualizing and Performing

Students who have difficulty with writing or with presenting their ideas orally can demonstrate their understanding of the novel in a variety of ways:

- making cluster diagrams or sketching their ideas

- creating tableaux showing where characters are in relation to one another during a scene, their poses or stances, and their facial expressions

- creating thought balloons with drawings or phrases that show what a character is thinking at a given moment

- drawing their own thoughts in thought balloons above a sketched self-portrait

- listing or drawing images that come to mind as they read or hear a certain section or passage of the novel

- making a comic-book version of the novel (with or without words)

- coming to class as a character in the novel

Bearstone

Assessment Options

Perhaps the most important goal of assessment is to inform instruction. As you monitor the degree to which your students understand and engage with the novel, you will naturally modify your instructional plan. The frequency and balance of class and small-group discussion, the time allowed for activities, and the extent to which direct teaching of reading skills and strategies, literary elements, or vocabulary is appropriate can all be planned on the basis of your ongoing assessment of your students' needs.

Several forms of assessment are particularly appropriate for work with the novel:

Observing and note taking Anecdotal records that reflect both the degree and the quality of students' participation in class and small-group discussions and activities will help you target areas in which coaching or intervention is appropriate. Because communication skills are such an integral part of working with the novel in a classroom setting, it is appropriate to evaluate the process of making meaning in this social context.

Involving yourself with dialogue journals and letters You may want to exchange notes with students instead of, or in addition to, encouraging them to keep reader's logs. A powerful advantage of this strategy is that at the same time you have the opportunity to evaluate students' responses, you can make a significant difference in the quality of the response. When students are aware that their comments are valued (and addressed to a real audience, an audience that writes back), they often wake up to the significance of what they are reading and begin to make stronger connections between the text and their own lives.

Agreeing on criteria for evaluation If evaluation is to be fair, it must be predictable. As students propose and plan an activity or project, collaborate with them to set up the criteria by which their work will be evaluated, and be consistent in applying only those criteria.

Encouraging self-evaluation and goal setting When students are partners with you in creating criteria for evaluation, they can apply those criteria to their own work. You might ask them to rate themselves on a simple scale of 1, 2, or 3 for each of the criteria and to arrive at an overall score. Students can then set goals based on self-evaluation.

Peer evaluation Students can participate in evaluating one another's demonstrations and presentations, basing their evaluations upon a previously established set of standards. Modeling a peer-evaluation session will help students learn this method, and a chart or checklist can guide peer discussion. Encourage students to be objective, sensitive, courteous, and constructive in their comments.

Keeping portfolios If you are in an environment where portfolios contain only carefully chosen samples of students' writing, you may want to introduce a second, "working," portfolio and negotiate grades with students after examining all or selected items from these portfolios.

Opportunities for Assessment

The suggestions in this Study Guide provide multiple opportunities for assessment across a range of skills:

- demonstrating reading comprehension
- keeping reader's logs
- listening and speaking
- working in groups—both discussion and activity-oriented
- planning, developing, and presenting a final project
- acquiring vocabulary
- taking tests

Questions for Self-evaluation and Goal Setting

- What are the three most important things I learned in my work with this novel?
- How will I follow up with these so that I remember them?
- What was the most difficult part of working with this novel?
- How did I deal with the difficulty, and what would I do differently?
- What two goals will I work toward in my [reading/writing/group work, etc.]?
- What steps will I take to achieve those goals?

Items for a "Working" Portfolio

- reading records
- drafts of written work and project plans
- audio- and videotapes of presentations
- notes on discussions
- reminders of cooperative projects, such as planning and discussion notes
- artwork
- objects and mementos connected with themes and topics in the novel
- other evidence of engagement with the book

For help with establishing and maintaining portfolio assessment, examine the **Portfolio Management System** *in* **Elements of Literature.**

About the Writer

Will Hobbs

More on Hobbs

"Hobbs, Will." ***Something about the Author,*** Volume 72, pp. 110–111. Detroit: Gale Research, 1993. A brief sketch with an interesting sidelight.

McKinney, Caroline S. "Will Hobbs." ***Authors & Artists,*** Volume 14, pp. 135–141. Detroit: Gale Research, 1995. An extensive analysis of Hobbs and his writing.

Also by Hobbs

Beardance. New York: Atheneum, 1993. In this sequel to *Bearstone,* Cloyd returns to the mountains with Walter and helps two grizzly bear cubs survive the death of their mother.

Changes in Latitude. New York: Avon Flare, 1994. A cocky teenager changes during a family trip to Mexico as he becomes aware of his parents' difficulties and his brother's interest in saving endangered species.

Downriver. New York: Atheneum, 1991. A group of rebellious adolescents steals its leader's equipment and runs the perilous white water at the bottom of the Grand Canyon.

Far North. New York: William Morrow, 1996. After their plane and its pilot plunge over a waterfall, two teenagers and an elderly American Indian hunter are stranded in the Canadian wilderness.

Ghost Canoe. New York: William Morrow, 1997. While fishing in the Pacific Northwest, fourteen-year-old Nathan MacAllister finds clues to lost treasure and a sea captain's murder.

River Thunder. New York: Bantam, 1997. In this sequel to *Downriver,* Troy, Jessie, and their friends face new challenges as they run the rapids of the Grand Canyon's Colorado River.

A biography of Will Hobbs appears in Bearstone, HRW Library *edition. You may wish to share this additional biographical information with your students.*

When Will Hobbs was a child, his older brother locked himself in his room to get some privacy from the large, boisterous Hobbs family. Will flushed him out with a stink bomb. A few years later, when Will became a teenager, he understood his brother's need for privacy. He discovered that adolescence is a time of great change, a struggle for survival that requires time alone. The characters in Hobbs's novels often face loneliness and great challenges in their struggles to survive.

Since Will's father was in the Air Force, the family traveled to many interesting—and isolated—places. Will was born in Pittsburgh, Pennsylvania, in 1947; before he could walk, however, the family had moved to the Panama Canal Zone. After that, his new homes included Virginia, Alaska, California, and Texas. Scouting sparked Will's interest in the outdoors, and the five Hobbs children camped, hiked, fished, and backpacked in many different regions. Their outdoor adventures helped shape Will's writing.

Although Will has traveled to many beautiful places, the American Southwest has captured his imagination the most. In 1973, Will and his wife Jean moved to southwest Colorado. They currently live in a rock house Will built near Durango. The couple enjoys watching black bears, coyotes, badgers, and elk. The desert wilderness allows Will time to hike through, write about, and explore his own "desert" places.

About the Novel

Bearstone

In an interview in *The Horn Book Magazine,* Will Hobbs noted that *Bearstone* arose from a real event—one of the "last" grizzly bears in Colorado was killed in the San Juan Mountains in 1979. The news spread because another bear—one people had presumed was the "last" grizzly in Colorado—had been killed twenty-seven years earlier.

CRITICAL COMMENT

> Despite his strong motivation to write about this incident, it took Hobbs eight years—and six drafts—to complete *Bearstone*. According to George Gleason, Hobbs's hard work paid off. In *School Library Journal,* Gleason wrote: "Extremely well-drawn characters, vivid incidents in and around the mountains of the Continental Divide, and powerful yet sensitive moments between the boy and the old man put this far above other coming-of-age stories."

Some aspects of the novel may provoke controversy. One of the conflicts in the text is hunting for sport versus hunting for food. Walter's friend Rusty leads groups into the mountains for the thrill of tracking and killing bears and for the pleasure of adding trophies to their collections. Cloyd identifies with the bears and is sickened at the unnecessary killing.

In addition, Cloyd courts danger. He often travels by hitchhiking, a risky undertaking that is compounded by the fact that hitchhiking puts him out of contact with his guardians for extended periods of time.

Awards and Honors

Notable Book,
Children's Book Council

Best Book for Young Adults, American Library Association

Teachers' Choice Award, International Reading Association

Regional Book Award,
Mountains and Plains Booksellers Association

Spur Award,
Western Writers of America

Colorado Book Award

For Listening

Bearstone. Recorded Books, 1996. A recording of the full text of *Bearstone*.

Key Elements

Bearstone

Make a Connection

Have you ever been so angry that you did something that you regretted later? What did you do to improve the situation?

Plot

Chapters 1–8 Fourteen-year-old Cloyd Atcitty has had a rough life: his mother died at his birth, he has never met his father, and he has failed his classes. He runs away from a group home to find his father, but the older man is lying brain-dead in a hospital. Cloyd is taken to a Colorado ranch owned by Walter Landis, an elderly widower who has lost much of his interest in life since the death of his wife. Near the farm, in an ancient burial site, Cloyd finds a tiny turquoise stone shaped like a bear, an animal of symbolic power to the Utes. He picks out one of Walter's horses and names it "Blueboy." Then he starts building a fence on Walter's property, determined to prove his worth. Cloyd also meets Walter's friend, the bear hunter Rusty.

Chapters 9–15 Cloyd sets the fenceposts, but when he sees Rusty's hunting party return with a dead bear, his anger erupts. He saws through each of Walter's peach trees and half of the fifty-seven fenceposts he had set. Furious, Walter drives Cloyd back to the group home. On the way, however, he examines the bearstone and understands Cloyd's pain. Walter instead takes Cloyd to his grandmother's home in Utah. Realizing his errors, Cloyd returns to Walter, and they exchange apologies. They decide to reopen Walter's mine in the Weminuche Wilderness Area. On the way, Cloyd gets caught in a storm while fishing, suffers from hypothermia, stumbles into a campsite, and is saved by a stranger.

Chapters 16–22 Cloyd sets out to explore a nearby mountain, the Rio Grande Pyramid. On the mountain, Blueboy falls into deep mud and risks death rather than injure Cloyd. Amazingly, the horse is unharmed. Cloyd reaches the peak, performs a Ute ceremony, and spots a bear. When Cloyd tells Walter and Rusty about the bear, Rusty decides to kill the animal. Cloyd tries to save it, but he arrives too late. Rusty realizes that he has killed a grizzly, which is illegal. Rusty reports the kill but claims that it was in self-defense. When Cloyd finds Walter badly injured in a mining accident, he saves Walter's life by intercepting the helicopter sent to pick up the bear carcass. In doing so, he resists the urge to get revenge on Rusty. Cloyd decides to stay with Walter on the ranch and replaces the peach trees that he destroyed.

Key Elements (continued)

Bearstone

Plot Structure

The **major conflict** around which the plot is built is Cloyd's **internal conflict** over who he really is and how to reconcile his heritage with the problems and choices of adolescence.

The **resolution** of this conflict is Cloyd's choice not to return to his family but to take care of Walter.

The **climax** of the story in terms of the high point of the action takes place in the mountains when Cloyd sees Rusty kill the grizzly and then discovers Walter's accident. Another important turning point comes when Cloyd must choose between fulfilling his long-held desire to return to White Mesa or staying in Colorado to care for Walter.

In the denouement, Cloyd and Walter begin to build a new life, "living a good way."

A series of minor conflicts, both internal and external, move the plot forward at the same time they develop the novel's themes. Among these conflicts are

- Cloyd's internal conflict between his affection and gratitude toward Walter and his anger at Walter for being friendly to bear hunters
- the conflict between Walter and Cloyd over Cloyd's destruction of the peach orchard and the fence posts
- Cloyd's conflict with Walter's friend Rusty over whether the bears should be killed (Rusty) or whether their lives should be respected (Cloyd)
- Walter's internal conflict over whether to keep the farm going or return to his mine

Theme

Students will see the following **themes,** or main ideas, developed in detail in *Bearstone*.

Growing from Adversity When Cloyd returns to Walter after running away from the farm, Walter tells him, " . . . the hurt you get over makes you stronger." Cloyd feels remorse for destroying the fenceposts he set up earlier and the peach trees that Walter's wife once planted. The trees represent Walter's love for his wife and for the home they made together. The **symbol** becomes more poignant when one remembers that Walter, a widower, struggles to cope with his wife's death. Nonetheless, Walter is able to forgive Cloyd and show him compassion. Walter's love enables Cloyd to overcome his feeling of being betrayed by Walter and to help Walter

---

Make a Connection

Ask students to describe what their heritage means to them. Have them describe cultural events, customs, or objects that mean something special to them.

Connecting with Elements of Literature

You can use *Bearstone* to extend students' examination of the themes and topics presented in *Elements of Literature*.

- *Introductory Course:* "All Creatures Great and Small," Collection Four
- *First Course:* "Who Am I?" Collection Two
- *Second Course:* " From Generation to Generation, " Collection Two

Study Guide | 9

Key Elements (continued)   *Bearstone*

dig gold in his mine, The Pride of the West. Later in the novel, Cloyd builds on this new maturity to overcome the pain of seeing the outfitter Rusty kill the grizzly bear. "It was all part of learning what it meant to live in a good way," Cloyd realizes, recalling the words of his grandmother.

The Importance of Heritage Cloyd is deeply attuned to the rhythms of nature—the mountains, canyons, weather, and animals. He can catch a trout with his bare hands and climb steep mountains with assurance. Cloyd is so close to nature that he feels "a part of it all, like the beating heart of the mountains is your own heart." Cloyd is rooted to the ways of the Utes. His grandmother has brought him up to be respectful to the Ancient Ones. Cloyd treats with respect the buried infant he finds. Cloyd's grandmother has also encouraged him to live in a good way. Cloyd decides to work hard, to take care of Walter, and to put aside vengeful feelings. Part of living in a good way is to enjoy nature and to treat it with respect.

Characters

Students will meet the following major **characters** in *Bearstone*.

Cloyd Atcitty is a fourteen-year-old Ute who has grown up illiterate and without parents. Hobbs tells us, "His limbs were rounded, undefined, and he was chunky overall in the way of Ute men." Long, shiny black hair frames Cloyd's large, round face. Sullen at the novel's start, Cloyd comes to realize the meaning of forgiveness and compassion and learns to draw on his inner strengths.

Walter Landis, a kindly widowed rancher, takes Cloyd in and teaches him about mining, the mountains, love, and forgiveness. He becomes a father to Cloyd, both spiritually and emotionally.

Rusty, a hunting guide, is called "the best outfitter in the San Juans." Cloyd feels that Rusty humiliates him. Rusty tracks and kills a grizzly bear.

Susan James is the concerned housemother of the group home for boys where Cloyd lived for a time. Susan brings Cloyd to live with Walter, a longtime friend of hers.

Leeno Atcitty, Cloyd's father, lies brain-dead in an Arizona hospital.

Grandmother, Cloyd's maternal grandmother, It a Ute who is steeped in the ancient traditions of her people.

Make a Connection

Ask students whether they have ever known an elderly person who has lost a spouse. Have them discuss how the widow or widower responded to that loss.

---

10 | *Bearstone*

Key Elements (continued)

Bearstone

Setting

The American Southwest is crucial to *Bearstone*: It both reflects Cloyd's heritage and aids in his maturation. Cloyd hates the group home in Durango, Colorado, in part because it has isolated him from his roots in White Mesa, Utah. Cloyd is initially happy at Walter's ranch, near Durango, the Ute ancestral homeland. Later, at the Rio Grande Pyramid, Cloyd affirms his connection to the land and to his heritage: "He'd never felt this way before, free and peaceful at the same time."

Point of View

Bearstone is told from the **omniscient point of view,** in which the **narrator** knows everything about the characters and their problems. The book focuses primarily on what Cloyd thinks and feels, but it also features Walter's thoughts and emotions.

Figures of Speech

Explain to students that **figurative language** is not meant to be understood as literally true. At times, however, it can enhance a reader's understanding and enjoyment in ways that literal language cannot. **Figures of speech** involve an imaginative comparison between seemingly unlike things. As such, figures of speech use words in fresh, new ways to appeal to the imagination. The most common figures of speech found in *Bearstone* are the **simile,** the **metaphor,** and **personification.** These figures of speech often focus on nature or invoke American Indian culture. They complement the subject matter and the tone of the book.

In Chapter 5, for example, Hobbs uses the simile "Like thousands of knives, the dark walls were flinty and jagged, so unlike the smooth sandstones of home."

In Chapter 10, Hobbs uses a metaphor to compare Cloyd's emotional upheaval to an unexpected rainstorm: "With the suddenness of a cloudburst in the desert, tears ran down his face."

Hobbs uses personification in Chapter 6, which closes with Walter's claim that the tops of the mountains are so high that they can "punch holes in the sky."

Make a Connection

Have students locate on a map some of the places mentioned in the novel. If students know this part of the Southwest, have them describe it.

Make a Connection

Explain that in the **first-person point of view,** the **narrator** is one of the **characters** in the story, and readers see events through the narrator's eyes. Discuss how *Bearstone* might be different if it were told in the first-person point of view—and who the narrator might be.

A **Literary Elements Worksheet** that focuses on figures of speech appears on page 36 of this Study Guide.

Study Guide | 11

Key Elements (continued)

Bearstone

Make a Connection

Think of movies you have seen where an event has been foreshadowed. Recall the **foreshadowing** and what it foretold.

*A **Literary Elements Worksheet** that focuses on foreshadowing appears on page 37 of this Study Guide.*

Foreshadowing

By dropping clues or hints about upcoming events in a narrative, writers use **foreshadowing** to build **suspense** or **tension** for the reader. Foreshadowing also helps writers link related details. For example, at the end of Chapter 2, Hobbs foreshadows Cloyd's maturation when he says, "Sliding off the rock, Cloyd slipped through the orchard and vanished among the tall trees, then began to climb. He didn't know he was climbing toward a treasure and a turning point. He wanted only to reach that piece of desert in the sky." Cloyd's maturation is the "turning point"; his relationship with Walter and his newfound adulthood are the "great treasure."

Before You Read

Bearstone

Activities

BUILDING ON PRIOR KNOWLEDGE

A Friend in Need

Work in a small group with two other students and consider this situation:

> A fourteen-year-old boy has been placed in a group home because his parents are dead and his grandmother is unable to care for him. The teenager can barely read. He is failing all his subjects. He keeps running away from the group home. How would you help this boy?

Discuss the problem, list possible solutions, explain why each solution would be effective, and pick the one that is most effective.

MAKING PERSONAL CONNECTIONS

Who Am I?

The main **character** in *Bearstone*, Cloyd Atcitty, is a Ute. Utes, traditionally, consider bears to embody many important qualities. Select an animal that you think represents you. Then, write a brief paragraph explaining why you are like this animal. Use specific details.

MAKING PREDICTIONS

Riddle Me This

Will Hobbs coined (made up) the term *bearstone* and used it for the title of his novel. Write a brief paragraph predicting the title's meaning and what you think might happen in the book. Refer to your predictions as you read.

SPECULATING

Crime and Punishment

The main character in the novel, fourteen-year-old Cloyd Atcitty, will have the chance to get revenge. As a class, discuss how revenge differs from justice, what anger does to the person who seeks revenge, and what complications might arise as a result of obtaining revenge. Then, speculate on the kinds of questions you might ask yourself before deciding whether to take revenge.

Novel Notes

Use **Novel Notes, Issue 1**

- to find out more about some of the topics and themes in *Bearstone*
- to get ideas for writing activities and other projects that will take you deeper into the book

Study Guide | 13

Chapters 1–8

Bearstone

Making Meanings

First Thoughts

1. Do you like Cloyd? Would you want him as a friend? Why or why not?

Shaping Interpretations

2. Why does Cloyd want to see his father, Leeno Atcitty?

3. What do you think Walter's peach trees **symbolize,** or represent, in the novel?

4. How does Cloyd show his respect for the Ancient Ones?

5. How does Cloyd's secret name suit him?

6. Who is Rusty? How does Cloyd feel about him?

> **READING CHECK**
>
> a. Why can't Cloyd go home to his grandmother for the summer, even though he very much wants to return to her?
> b. Why does Walter take such good care of his peach trees?
> c. What two things does Cloyd find in the cave on the cliff?
> d. What secret name does Cloyd give himself?

Connecting with the Text

7. Cloyd works hard to dig the postholes—so hard that he surprises himself. Think of a time when you surprised yourself by some personal success. How did your reasons for wanting to succeed compare with Cloyd's?

Extending the Text

8. Walter's wife used to say that "a ranch was like a house, but a farm was a home." What do you think makes a house into a home?

Challenging the Text

9. Explain what the **title** Bearstone means. Do you think it is a fitting title for this novel? If you could give the novel a different title based on what you've read so far, what would it be, and why?

Chapters 1–8 *(continued)*

Bearstone

Choices: Building Your Portfolio

BUILDING A WORD LIST

Word Exchange

Which words in these chapters are unfamiliar to you? Divide these chapters among yourself and three classmates, with each of you taking two chapters. On your own, each of you should make a list of about ten unfamiliar words. Then, use a dictionary to define each word. When you gather again, teach each other the new words. Test your knowledge by using the words in original sentences.

SOUNDTRACK

Setting the Mood

Imagine these chapters as part of a movie, complete with a soundtrack. Either alone or with a partner, choose some music that could serve as a background for any **scene** in Chapters 1–8 of *Bearstone*. You could choose part of the soundtrack of a movie that reminds you of the scene, select a piece of classical music that captures the scene's mood or find a popular song that expresses the emotions that a character in the scene feels. Play the music for the class, and explain how it fits the scene.

CREATIVE WRITING

Letters from Home

Try writing the letter that Cloyd's sister has sent to him. Include her feelings about Cloyd, about school, and about their separation. If you wish, save your finished letter in your writing portfolio.

Consider This . . .

Sliding off the rock, Cloyd slipped through the orchard and vanished among the tall trees, then began to climb. He didn't know he was climbing toward a treasure and a turning point. He wanted only to reach that piece of desert in the sky.

What "treasure" and "turning point" do you think Cloyd will reach? Toward what are *you* climbing?

Writing Follow-up: Reflecting

Think about a time when you made a decision, realized something important to you, or achieved a goal. Describe the events that led to this turning point.

Novel Notes

Use **Novel Notes, Issue 2**

- to find out more about some of the topics and themes in Chapters 1–8
- to get ideas for writing activities and other projects related to *Bearstone*

Study Guide

Chapters 9–15

Bearstone

Making Meanings

First Thoughts

1. What do you think of Walter's explosion of anger toward Cloyd? Do your feelings toward Walter change over the chapters that follow? Explain.

Shaping Interpretations

2. After Cloyd destroys Walter's peach trees, why doesn't Walter smash Cloyd's bearstone?

3. Why does Cloyd decide to return to Walter's ranch after Walter drives him to his grandmother's house?

4. Why does Cloyd tell Walter his secret name and the history of the bearstone?

> **READING CHECK**
>
> a. Why does Cloyd cut the peach trees only part of the way through rather than completely through?
> b. Back on the reservation, what does Cloyd's grandmother want to know about Walter?
> c. Where do Walter and Cloyd stop on their way to The Pride of the West, Walter's gold mine? Why?
> d. What plan does Walter come up with to allow Cloyd to go to the Rio Grande Pyramid alone?

5. What does Cloyd learn when he nearly dies in the hailstorm? How does he change as a result of this experience?

6. Why is it so important for Cloyd to climb the Rio Grande Pyramid?

Connecting with the Text

7. Cloyd is only fourteen years old. Do you think Walter was right to let him climb the Rio Grande Pyramid alone? Would you undertake a journey like this yourself? Why or why not?

Extending the Text

8. Do you think that Walter will find gold in his mine? Why or why not?

Challenging the Text

9. Will Hobbs uses many technical terms for the action and landscape described in the novel—for example, *assay, carbide, geode,* and *ramada.* In your opinion, do these words add to or detract from the novel? Explain.

Chapters 9–15 (continued)

Bearstone

Choices: Building Your Portfolio

READER'S THEATER

The Play's the Thing
With a few classmates, select a dramatic **scene** from Chapters 9–15 and prepare it as a Reader's Theater presentation. Look for a scene that has dramatic action, sharp conflict, and few characters. You probably will want to include a narrator; add simple costumes and props if you wish. Have someone videotape your presentation so that you can enjoy it later.

DISCUSSION

The Experts Speak
Review Chapters 9–15 with some classmates. Each member of your group should choose and study a literary element of this part of the novel. You could outline the **plot,** describe the **conflict** or **setting,** review the **characters** and what we learn about them, or identify **themes** suggested by this part of the story. Review that element of the novel until you feel like an "expert" on it. When you gather again, have each expert share what he or she has learned with the rest of the group.

MAP

The Road Taken
Create a map that traces the route that Cloyd has traveled thus far. Figure out about how much time it would have taken Cloyd to travel from place to place. From this information, decide which roads Cloyd probably traveled on and how fast he was going during each leg of his journey. As you continue to read, add details to the map to show Cloyd's complete journey.

CREATIVE WRITING

Live in a Good Way
Create a guidebook for living in a good way. Collect proverbs and sayings that you have heard. Add your own thoughts. If you like, add any drawings that would help illustrate a good way to live.

Consider This . . .
The pickup was small in the distance by the time he realized he'd lost something of priceless value. He waved forlornly, then furiously, as the truck vanished. With the suddenness of a cloudburst in the desert, tears ran down his face.

What has Cloyd lost? How do you think he might regain it? Have you ever lost something important? If so, what was your reaction to losing it?

Writing Follow-up: Problem Solving

Describe the problem Cloyd faces. What has he lost? Then, propose one or more solutions for how he could solve his problem.

Novel Notes

Use **Novel Notes, Issue 3**

- to find out more about some of the topics and themes in Chapters 9–15
- to get ideas for writing activities and other projects related to *Bearstone*

Study Guide | 17

Chapters 16–22

Bearstone

Making Meanings

First Thoughts

1. Do you think Cloyd did the right thing by coming to live with Walter at the end of the novel? Why or why not?

Shaping Interpretations

2. What do Blueboy's actions suggest about the relationship between the horse and Cloyd?

> **READING CHECK**
>
> **a.** How does Blueboy save Cloyd's life?
> **b.** What does Cloyd do when he reaches the peak of the Rio Grande Pyramid?
> **c.** What does Rusty discover after he kills the bear?
> **d.** What surprising gift does Cloyd buy for Walter at the story's end?

3. Why doesn't Cloyd turn Rusty in to the authorities after the trapper kills the bear?

4. Why does Cloyd give Walter his most treasured possession, the bearstone?

5. In what ways has Walter become a father to Cloyd?

6. What do you think the crack in the foundation of Walter's house **symbolizes,** or represents? Why is it significant that Cloyd repairs the crack at the end of the novel?

Connecting with the Text

7. At the end of the book, Cloyd is happy because he is no longer alone. Do you prefer to be alone or with others? How important are other people in your life?

Extending the Text

8. What other stories do you know of in which an older person and a younger person learn to appreciate each other? How do their relationships compare to the relationship between Walter and Cloyd?

Challenging the Text

9. Will Hobbs uses **foreshadowing** to hint at what will happen later in the story. Think about the end of Chapter 15, for example. There, Hobbs foreshadows the danger that Cloyd will face on the Rio Grande Pyramid by showing Walter's uneasy feelings about having Cloyd make the trip alone. Find another example of foreshadowing in the novel. Explain how it does or does not increase the novel's **suspense.**

Chapters 16–22 (continued)

Bearstone

Choices: Building Your Portfolio

CHARACTER ANALYSIS

Letting the Character Out of the Bag

Are you interested in what makes people "tick"? Do you enjoy looking at events from someone else's point of view? Show your understanding of some of the **characters** in *Bearstone* by making a "paper bag player" for Cloyd, Walter, Rusty, Cloyd's grandmother, or Susan James. On the outside of the bag, draw pictures that suggest what the character seems like to other people. Inside each bag, place small items or pictures that suggest the character's inner emotions, thoughts, and values. Find a classmate who chose the same character as you did. Compare the ways in which you represented him or her.

CREATIVE WRITING

I Am . . .

Writing as Cloyd, complete the following "I Am" poem. Use what you have learned about Cloyd to express his personality.

I Am

I am _____.
I wonder _____.
I hear _____.
I see _____.
I like _____.
I want _____.
I am _____!

TABLEAU

Frozen in Time

Work with some classmates to create a tableau. Choose a key scene from this last part of the novel, assign parts, have players position themselves in the scene, and "freeze" it in place. Then, have one student at a time "unfreeze" and speak in character. The student should explain what the **character** is thinking during the scene.

Consider This . . .

[Cloyd] wanted to tell him this is the heart of the mountains, up here in the light where you can see forever. Where you feel like you're a part of it all, like the beating heart of the mountains is your own heart.

What does Cloyd find at the peak of Rio Grande Pyramid that is so important to him? When have you ever felt that you were "a part of it all"?

Writing Follow-up: Comparing

Compare what the "heart of the mountains" means to Cloyd and Walter. Sum up by stating how the two view things differently.

Novel Notes

Use **Novel Notes, Issue 4**

- to find out more about some of the topics and themes in Chapters 16–22
- to get ideas for writing activities and other projects related to *Bearstone*

Novel Projects

Bearstone

Cross-Curricular Connections

MATHEMATICS
It's Home!
Research the history of American Indians in your state. What was the American Indian population before settlers came? What was it fifty years later? What is it now? Construct a bar graph to show your findings. In your class presentation, include information about what American Indian groups lived in your state and what happened when settlers came.

SOCIAL STUDIES
Respecting the Bear
Around the world, **legends** and **folk tales** are a part of people's cultures and oral traditions. Gather American Indian tales about bears. Read at least two to the class, and explain why you chose them and what truths or customs these tales illustrate.

HEALTH
A Chilling Situation
Cloyd wrestles with hypothermia when he is caught in a storm. Fortunately, a camper knows exactly what to do and how to save him. Create a manual that describes hypothermia, gives tips on how to avoid it, and tells what to do in case it sets in.

ART
The Milestone Book
At first, Cloyd is a painfully isolated, insecure teenager. By the end of the novel, however, he has become a far more self-assured young man, able to accept love and reject revenge. Make and share a scrapbook or memory book that shows (in types of artwork of your own choosing) several milestones, or key events, in Cloyd's life, as related in *Bearstone*.

Novel Projects (continued)

Bearstone

Multimedia and Internet Connections

NOTE: Check with your teacher about school policies on accessing Internet sites. If a Web site named here is not available, use key words to locate a similar site.

TELEVISION: NEWS STORY

We Interrupt This Program . . .

Imagine you are at the hospital just after Walter is brought in by helicopter. Form two teams. One team plays the roles of reporters who interview Cloyd, Rusty, the helicopter pilot, and the medical personnel to get the story for the evening news. The other team plays the roles of Cloyd, Rusty, the helicopter pilot, and the medical personnel. The reporters should plan what questions to ask each character. Rehearse the interviews. Then, act out your news story before the class, or videotape your story to present to the class.

RADIO: INTERVIEW

Our Guest Tonight

With two students, create a radio talk-show interview with two book reviewers. One of you should be the show host; the other two should be the reviewers. During the interview, the host finds out what each reviewer thinks of *Bearstone*. Possible interview questions: What did you learn from this book? Is there any part of it you object to? Is there anything about it you wish were different?

FILM: MOCK TRIAL

Accused!

Realizing that he has killed a grizzly bear, an animal protected by federal law, Rusty decides to lie and claim that the bear attacked him. Hold a mock trial to decide whether Rusty is telling the truth and, if not, how he should be punished. You might use a format from TV court shows. Act out your trial and, if possible, videotape it.

INTERNET: POSTING COMMENTS

Critical Review: *Bearstone*

Write a critical review of *Bearstone*. First, establish three criteria for a successful novel, such as dramatic plot, realistic characters, and interesting setting. Then, evaluate how well *Bearstone* measures up to these criteria. You may wish to consult other critical reviews of the novel, such as those that are available on the Internet at the Amazon Web site

http://www.amazon.com

When you have finished writing and revising, post your reviews—either at the Amazon Web site or, if possible, at your school's or local public library's Web site.

INTERNET: RESEARCH

Bear with Me

Bears are a link to Cloyd's heritage; furthermore, he admires their strength and majesty. Find out more about various kinds of bears around the world, including their habits and status as protected or endangered species. Work individually or in small groups to select types of bears or subtopics to research. You may find a wealth of information available from "The Bear Den" and "The Cub Den" on the Internet

http://www.nature-net.com/bears

or you may prefer to browse on your own. Present your findings to the class.

Study Guide **21**

Exploring the Connections

Making Meanings

Denning with the Great Bear

Novel Notes
See **Issue 5**

1. Think back to *Bearstone*. What new information about the novel did you learn from this essay?
2. What does the title of this essay mean? How does it relate to *Bearstone*?

> **READING CHECK**
> a. What got Hobbs started writing *Bearstone*?
> b. Where did he get the idea for *Beardance,* the sequel to *Bearstone*?

3. What do you think Hobbs means when he says that "there's a part of the human heart that longs for wild places"?
4. Inspired by nature, Will Hobbs found it very easy to write *Beardance.* What inspires you to do something creative, such as write, draw, dance, or sing?

---

the earth is a living thing
Baby Bear Moon
Here on This Mountain

Novel Notes
See **Issue 5**

1. Complete the following statements:
   - The earth seems alive to me because . . .
   - If I saw a bear, as the speaker in "Baby Bear Moon" mentions, I would . . .
   - If I were all alone on a mountain, I would feel . . .

> **READING CHECK**
> a. In the first stanza of "the earth is a living thing," to what is the earth compared?
> b. What advice is given in "Baby Bear Moon"?
> c. In "Here on This Mountain," what do the Last Great Warrior, the Last Young Maiden, the Buffalo, and the River have in common?

2. What **images** in "the earth is a living thing" explain the title?
3. How is Cloyd like the child in "Baby Bear Moon"?
4. How are the **speaker** in "Here on This Mountain" and Cloyd in *Bearstone* similar in what they have done? in how they feel?
5. In your opinion, how are these three poems alike? What ideas from *Bearstone* do they reflect?
6. In "Baby Bear Moon," a child is raised by bears. Do you think a human child could survive in the woods with wild animals? Why or why not?

22 | *Bearstone*

Exploring the Connections (continued)

Making Meanings
Dancer

1. How did you react at the end of the story? Were you surprised by the link between Clarissa and Molly Graybull? Explain.

2. Why does the narrator take Clarissa to the dance, even though the child tried to kill a cat a few days earlier?

3. Why is dancing so important to Clarissa?

4. In your opinion, what does Molly Graybull **symbolize,** or represent, in this story?

5. How are the **characters** of Clarissa and Cloyd similar at the start of their stories? How are they similar at the end?

6. Vickie Sears has chosen Clarissa's foster mother to be the **narrator** of the story. Do you think the story would be more effective if Clarissa were the narrator? Why or why not?

> **READING CHECK**
> Draw a storyboard or a cartoon that illustrates the main events in "Dancer." Include at least four events.

Lesson 1
Lesson 2

1. Talk with a partner about your responses to these poems. Start by completing the following statements:
   - In "Lesson 1," the desert reminded me of a(n) ...
   - In "Lesson 2," the ending seemed to tell me that ...
   - These poems made me think of *Bearstone* because ...

2. How does Mora **personify** the desert in "Lesson 1"? In other words, how does she make the desert seem like a human being? Name two ways.

3. In "Lesson 2," what do you think the "small, white fairies" are, and why do they dance?

4. How do these poems make you feel about the desert? Explain.

> **READING CHECK**
> a. Describe the weather in "Lesson 1."
> b. Where does "Lesson 2" take place?

Novel Notes
See **Issue 5**

Study Guide | **23**

Exploring the Connections (continued)

Making Meanings

My Friend Flicka

Novel Notes
See **Issue 6**

1. Were you surprised by the end of this story? Why or why not?

2. How are Kennie and Flicka alike at the beginning of the story? How are they similar to Cloyd at the beginning of *Bearstone*?

3. What **motivation,** or guiding reason, moves Mr. McLaughlin to give Kennie a colt? What does his action suggest about Mr. McLaughlin as a father and a husband?

4. What does Flicka's behavior suggest about the link between the horse and Kennie? What parallels can you see between Kennie with his Flicka and Cloyd with his Blueboy?

5. In your opinion, why is Flicka so important to Kennie?

6. Imagine yourself as Kennie's father. What would you have done when Flicka became ill?

> **READING CHECK**
> On your own or with a partner, review "My Friend Flicka." Write down seven or eight **plot** events that you think are important. Make sure that they are in the correct order.

The Name Game

1. Of the names mentioned in this selection, which one do you like the best? Why?

2. According to the customs described here, why are names so important?

3. What do African naming customs reveal about the culture?

4. Think about the name that Cloyd chooses for himself in *Bearstone*. How is it in keeping with the American Indian traditions that Meltzer describes?

5. If you could rename yourself, what name would you select, and why?

> **READING CHECK**
> a. According to some cultures' beliefs, how might your name make you ill?
> b. Explain the African naming ceremony in this selection.
> c. In the ancient tribal tradition of the Delawares, who named the children?

24 | *Bearstone*

Novel Notes

Issue 1

Introducing *BEARSTONE*

A PROUD HERITAGE

The fourteen-year-old main character in *Bearstone* comes from the Ute Reservation in southeast Utah and is a member of the Weminuche band within the Ute Nation.

Ute headquarters is located in Towaoc, Colorado, at the base of "Sleeping Ute Mountain." The mountain got its name because it looks like a sleeping man with his headdress to the north. According to legend, as the Great Warrior God battled evil, his feet formed the mountains and valleys. He was wounded and fell into a deep sleep. Blood from his wound became water, and from his pockets came rain clouds. It is alleged that the Great Warrior God continues to care for the Utes.

First Land, Then Loss

When gold was discovered at Pikes Peak in 1859, bloody battles erupted between the miners and the Utes over the land. In 1863, the U.S. government tried to convince the Utes to leave their land in Colorado and move to the "Four Corners"—the place where Utah, Colorado, New Mexico, and Arizona meet. Most Utes refused, but they still lost most of their land and had to resettle on a reservation.

In 1873, when valuable minerals were discovered in the San Juan Mountains, the Utes lost four million acres.

In 1887, Congress passed the General Allotment Act, giving 150 to 300 acres of land to each Ute. In 1910, however, the rest of the reservation was opened up to non-Indian homesteaders. The result was a loss of more tribal land and a lasting grief for many Utes.

FOR YOUR READER'S LOG

As you read *Bearstone*, jot down some questions that you would like to ask Cloyd about his heritage.

American Indian Writers
Louise Erdrich

Louise Erdrich is the daughter of a Chippewa mother and a German American father. Erdrich was raised near the Turtle Mountain Chippewa Reservation in North Dakota. She writes novels, poetry, and short stories about American Indian Life. Her novel *Love Medicine* won a National Book Critics Circle Award.

ASK *the Professor*

Dear Dr. I. Knoweverything,

I'll bet you don't know the answer to this one! How can someone born in the United States, of two American parents, have citizenship in two nations?

—Cool in Colorado

Dear Cool,

I wish they were all this easy! The person must be an American Indian. Want to know more? All tribes recognized by the U.S. government have governing bodies. Indians who belong to these tribes are members of their tribal nation and also citizens of the United States. Thus, they hold two citizenships.

Study Guide | **25**

Novel Notes

Issue 2

BEARSTONE Chapters 1–8

THE UTES TODAY

The Ute tribal lands are located on the Colorado plateau in a high-desert area with deep canyons carved through the mesas. The natural resources of the land provide the Utes with income from oil and gas wells, cattle, and farming. The tribe employs more than 900 people—Utes, other American Indians, and Anglos—in its businesses and programs. In fact, it is the second largest employer in the Four Corners area.

HORSE SENSE

Hooves thundering and mane flying, a galloping horse inspires thoughts of total freedom. For centuries, people have admired horses for their beauty, strength, speed, and spirit.

Horses were first tamed in Asia about 5,000 years ago. Around 1600, the Spanish brought horses with them into Ute lands. The Utes were the first American Indians to acquire horses. Horses provided great mobility and changed the Ute way of life forever.

There are now over 150 different breeds of horses. Some are swift runners, able to cover many miles without tiring. Draft horses such as Clydesdales, the largest and strongest of all horses, are used to pull heavy loads. Quarter horses, which can stop and turn quickly, are used as working horses on ranches. The swift Thoroughbreds are raced for sport.

FOR YOUR READER'S LOG

What connection do you see between Cloyd's secret name and his feelings about Blueboy, his horse?

The Word PLACE

What's in a Name?

American Indian cultures have their own naming customs. In some groups, a medicine man or an older relative of the father gives the newborn baby his or her name. A boy might be named after a special animal or an important physical quality. A descriptive word or phrase can be added, as in *Tall Bull*, *Spotted Wolf*, or *Little Hawk*. Baby girls might receive names that contain the word woman, such as *Owl Woman*, *Little Creek Woman*, or *Buffalo Calf Road Woman*.

Since American Indian names often have come from objects, they can be shown easily in pictographs.

Traditionally, American Indian women keep the names they have been given at birth. Men, however, often replace a birth name with a new name that describes their accomplishments.

Novel Notes

Issue 3

BEARSTONE Chapters 9–15

CELEBRATE!

Long ago, when the first thunder in the spring was heard, it was time for the Ute Bear Dance. Bands came from miles around, set up camp, and prepared for the dance. They had practiced during the long winter months.

How did the Bear Dance start? According to legend, two brothers were hunting when one of them saw a bear dancing and making a noise while clawing a tree. The first brother kept hunting, but the other brother watched the bear. The bear said, "Return to your people and teach them the dance and songs of the bear." The Bear Dance came to represent Ute strength, wisdom, and survival.

The Utes still hold a Bear Dance every spring. Female dancers select their partners by flipping their shawl fringe at the man of their choice. The women line up facing west. The men line up facing the women to the east. Dancers hold hands as they move back and forth to the music. The gathering lasts four days; then everyone joins in a feast.

FOR YOUR READER'S LOG

Have you ever owned something that you cared about? If so, describe it and write your feelings about it. Compare and contrast your feelings to the feelings that Cloyd seems to have about the bearstone.

Ask the Professor

Dear Dr. I. Knoweverything,
I'm confused. This summer, right in the middle of a thunderstorm, all this ice came down. What's the scoop?
—Iced up in Kansas

Dear Iced,
Don't get out your winter clothes—hail isn't sleet. It *is* frozen moisture, but with a difference. Unlike sleet, hail freezes inside the clouds that cause thunderstorms. The hailstones drop toward the ground, but winds can drive them back into the colder air. The hailstones freeze again and again. Often the hailstones that finally hit the ground are tiny, but the largest hailstone on record, which fell in your state in 1970, weighed 1.7 pounds!

What's Cookin'?
FRYBREAD

In a mixing bowl, combine the first four ingredients and knead until smooth. Rub 1 tablespoon of oil over the dough. Cover and let it sit for about half an hour. Then tear off handfuls of dough, roll each into a ball, and pat them out in a circle to fit in the palm of your hand.

Fry the circles in hot oil. This recipe makes 10–12 frybreads. They can be eaten plain, but they also taste great with cinnamon sugar or with honey. Some people top frybread with ground meat, beans, lettuce, and tomatoes.

FRYBREAD INGREDIENTS
- 3 cups flour
- 2 teaspoons baking powder
- 1 teaspoon salt
- 1 1/2 cups warm water or milk
- 1 tablespoon oil or shortening
- oil or shortening for deep frying

Study Guide | 27

Novel Notes

Issue 4

BEARSTONE Chapters 16–22

PEACHY FACTS

- Peaches are a member of the rose family.
- Around the world, the peach is the third most popular deciduous tree fruit, right after the apple and the pear.
- The United States produces more peaches than any other country—20% of the world's peach supply. Italy, France, Greece, and Spain also grow major peach crops.
- To the ancient Chinese, the peach was a significant item in the fruit basket. Not only was it delicious, but it symbolized eternal life and love. People placed bowls of peaches in the tombs of loved ones. They also exchanged peaches as tokens of affection, as we might exchange roses.

FOR YOUR READER'S LOG

Standing on top of the Rio Grande Pyramid, Cloyd feels he is atop "the heart of the mountains, up here in the light where you can see forever." As you read, make a list of boundaries or barriers that have existed for Cloyd. Think about how he has broken through many of them during the story.

Explore the Divide

One of the most spectacular natural boundaries is the Continental Divide, also called the Great Divide. It is the mountain ridge that divides the streams flowing east toward the Atlantic Ocean and those flowing west toward the Pacific Ocean. The Continental Divide follows the crest of the Rocky Mountains and continues south into Mexico along the crest of the Sierra Madres.

The Word PLACE

Speaking Ute

American Indian languages have contributed many words to American English: food names like *pecan, hominy,* and *squash;* animal names, such as *chipmunk, raccoon, possum, skunk,* and *moose.* Many words reflecting American Indian lifestyles have entered English, too, including *totem, papoose, moccasin,* and *tomahawk.*

The Ute language is part of the "Uto-Aztecan" language family which reaches south into Mexico, west into Nevada and California, north into Wyoming and Idaho, and southeast into Oklahoma.

Here's a quick Ute language lesson.

Ute	English
Noochew	Ute People
Nooch	Ute Person
Mique Wush Tagooven	Hello, my friend
Pooneekay	
Vatsoom Ahdtuih	I'll see you again
Tuhaye	Good
Tograyock	Thank you

28 | Bearstone

Novel Notes

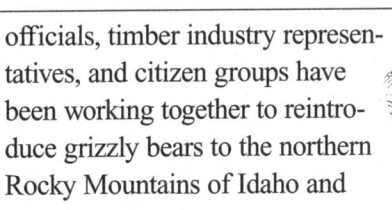

BEARSTONE Connections

IT'S NOT JUST THE DINOSAURS

Passenger pigeons and dodo birds will never take flight again. These animals have become extinct—they're gone from the earth.

Extinction is a natural process. Fossils reveal that thousands and thousands of animals that once lived on earth are now extinct. It's nobody's fault; people had nothing to do with their disappearance. In the last 400 years, however, the pace of extinction has increased. Since 1600, more than thirty different species of mammals have become extinct, and over a hundred more are in danger of vanishing. Threatened species, such as the grizzly bear, are abundant in certain parts of the world but are declining overall. Today, at least 80 percent of all endangered animals are in trouble because of people's deliberate actions or insensitivity toward them.

If you think that only rare and unusual animals are in danger of becoming extinct, think again!

Connections

- *Denning with the Great Bear*
- *the earth is a living thing*
- *Baby Bear Moon*
- *Here on This Mountain*
- *Lesson 1*
- *Lesson 2*

ANIMALS ON THE ENDANGERED SPECIES LIST

Asian elephant	**gorilla**	**golden parakeet**
cheetah	**gray bat**	**tiger**
American crocodile	**Tasmanian forester kangaroo**	**gray whale**
northern swift fox	**Asiatic lion**	**humpback whale**

Ask *the Professor*

Dear Dr. I. Knoweverything,
I've just read a great book called **Bearstone,** *and I want to know what's being done to save grizzly bears. Anything I can do?*
—It's a Bear

Dear Bear,
You bet things are being done to help grizzlies! First, they are on the "Threatened Species List" everywhere in the United States except Alaska and Hawaii. ("Threatened" species are not as near to extinction as "endangered" species are.) In addition, scientists, government officials, timber industry representatives, and citizen groups have been working together to reintroduce grizzly bears to the northern Rocky Mountains of Idaho and Montana.

In 1973, the United States government passed the Endangered Species Act to help protect animals in danger of extinction. In 1992, an international attempt to help rescue endangered species went into effect—the Biodiversity Treaty.

What can you do? Find out about local habitats that are in danger. Join a conservation organization. If you want to help, you won't have to look far!

FOR YOUR READER'S LOG

In your Reader's Log, write these authors' names: Will Hobbs, Lucille Clifton, Joseph Bruchac and Jonathan London, Nancy Wood, and Pat Mora. As you read their work, note one idea each writer suggests about nature.

Study Guide | **29**

Novel Notes

Issue 6

BEARSTONE Connections

Class Writing Pays!

For a writing-class assignment, a woman decided to write a story about a boy and a horse. She had lived on a ranch in Wyoming and knew the strong bonds that can develop between people and horses.

Her story created a sensation in class. She titled it "My Friend Flicka," published it, and then expanded it into a novel. A movie was made from the novel, and the woman, Mary O'Hara, wrote two more books about Ken and horses, *Thunderhead* and *Green Grass of Wyoming*.

Connection

- *My Friend Flicka*

IT'S A TOUGH LIFE

When is the time to start training a horse? Experts say that training should start at birth.

To get a foal used to being touched, trainers stroke and brush its thick, fuzzy coat often. By the time the horse is a month old, it has gotten used to wearing a halter. At one year, it learns to respond to reins; by age two, it is trained to wear a saddle.

At age three, training focuses on the work the horse will do—maybe as a riding horse, a racehorse, a polo pony, or even a circus horse. Within two more years, the horse is working full time. On the average, horses live about twenty-five to thirty years, so it's a working life.

The Word PLACE

Straight from the Horse's Mouth

bridle: harness used for guiding a horse

canter: slow gallop

colt: young male horse

foal: baby horse

gallop: the fastest gait of a horse

gee: command to make a horse turn right

halter: rope used to lead a horse

hand: measurement used to determine the height of a horse; one hand equals four inches

haw: command to make a horse turn left

mare: female horse

pony: a small horse

stallion: male horse

trot: slow walk

yearling: one-year-old horse

FOR YOUR READER'S LOG

Why does Kennie want a horse of his own so much? As you read "My Friend Flicka," make a word web to show how Kennie feels about Flicka.

Name _____

Reading Skills and Strategies Worksheet
Novel Organizer *Bearstone*

CHARACTER

Use the chart below to keep track of the characters in this book. Each time you come across a new character, write the character's name and the number of the page on which the character first appears. Then, jot down a brief description. Add information about the characters as you read. Put a star next to the name of each main character.

NAME OF CHARACTER	PAGE	DESCRIPTION

Study Guide | 31

Name _____

Reading Skills and Strategies Worksheet

Novel Organizer *(continued)* — *Bearstone*

SETTING

Where and when does this story take place? ....
....
....

CONFLICT (Read at least one chapter before you answer.)

What is the biggest problem faced by the main character(s)? ....
....
....

How do you predict it will be resolved? ....
....
....

MAJOR EVENTS

- ....
- ....
- ....
- ....
- ....

OUTCOME

How is the main problem resolved? (How accurate was your prediction?) ....
....
....

32 | *Bearstone*

Name _____ Date _____

Reading Skills and Strategies Worksheet
Bearstone

Chapters 1–8: Charting Causes and Effects

A **cause** is what makes something happen. The **effect** is what happens. Recognizing causes and effects can help you understand events in a novel and what they mean. For example, because his mother died, his father left, and his grandmother couldn't see to all his needs, Cloyd was sent to a group home. Because of his severe injuries in a car accident, Cloyd's father was brain-dead in a hospital.

Complete the following cause-and-effect chart. It will help you think about what Cloyd does in this first part of *Bearstone* and why he does it.

CAUSE	EFFECT
1. Cloyd fails all his subjects and runs away from the group home.	
2. Walter's wife dies.	
3. Cloyd finds the bearstone.	
4. Cloyd was taught to respect the Old Ways.	
5. Walter gives Cloyd a horse.	
	6. Cloyd builds a fence.
	7. Cloyd likes Walter.
	8. Cloyd is ashamed and angry.
	9. Cloyd doesn't like Rusty.
	10. Cloyd won't help with the hay.

Study Guide | **33**

Name _____ Date _____

Reading Skills and Strategies Worksheet
Bearstone

Chapters 9–15: Completing a Story Triangle

You can use a story triangle to keep track of several story details. Follow the directions to fill out this story triangle for *Bearstone*. Use what you know so far to give as much information as you can. (You may want to wait until the end of the novel to complete it.) Be creative as you choose words, phrases, and statements.

1. Name the main **character.**

2. Write two words that describe the main character.

3. Write three words that describe the **setting.**

4. Write four words that state one problem.

5. Write five words that describe the problem.

6. Write six words that state a second problem.

7. Write seven words that state a third problem.

8. Write eight words that describe the solution.

_____
1.

_____ _____
2.

_____ _____ _____
3.

_____ _____ _____ _____
4.

_____ _____ _____ _____ _____
5.

_____ _____ _____ _____ _____ _____
6.

_____ _____ _____ _____ _____ _____ _____
7.

_____ _____ _____ _____ _____ _____ _____ _____
8.

34 | *Bearstone*

Name _____ Date _____

Reading Skills and Strategies Worksheet
Bearstone

Chapters 16–22: Using a Time Line

You can use a time line to track the key events in a story, play, or novel. Complete the following time line to show eight of the most important events in Chapters 16–22 of *Bearstone*, in the order in which they take place.

CHAPTER 16

1. _____
2. _____
3. _____
4. _____
5. _____
6. _____
7. _____
8. _____

CHAPTER 22

Look back at all the events you listed. Which event do you think is most important? Write the event here and explain why you selected it.

....
....
....
....
....
....
....

Study Guide | **35**

Name _____ Date _____

Literary Elements Worksheet

Bearstone

Figures of Speech

Figures of speech are words or phrases that describe one thing in terms of another. They are not meant to be understood literally.

- A **simile** is a figure of speech that compares two unlike things, using the word *like* or *as* to make the comparison.
- A **metaphor** also compares two unlike things, but it does not use *like* or *as* to make the comparison.
- **Personification** gives human characteristics to nonhuman objects.

Here are ten figures of speech from *Bearstone*. Identify each one as a simile, a metaphor, or personification. Item 5 contains two types of figures of speech.

EXAMPLES	FIGURES OF SPEECH
1. He let himself sink into sleep like a heavy stone plunging into a well.	
2. You look like something the cat spit out.	
3. This mountain, it's like it blinked while I went off a young man, looks again and sees me ridin' back plumb aged.	
4. He'd been there so long he was like an old tree too deeply rooted for transplanting.	
5. Where you feel like you're a part of it all, like the beating heart of the mountains is your own heart.	
6. Peaks everywhere, dancing, jutting up, all in motion.	
7. …a room having no doors, its furniture and draperies the fantastic shapes of glistening, crystalline gold.	
8. …rivers bound for different oceans started out within spitting distance of each other.	
9. Like a rabbit in the sagebrush, Cloyd was into the room.	
10. He drifted deeper and deeper into the dark, like a leaf settling into the bottom of a deep pool.	

36 | *Bearstone*

Name _____ Date _____

Literary Elements Worksheet

Bearstone

Foreshadowing

A writer who uses **foreshadowing** will drop clues or hints to suggest events that will occur later in a plot. Realizing that "something is going to happen" adds to the feeling of **suspense** or **tension** in many novels, including *Bearstone*.

Below are five examples of foreshadowing from *Bearstone*. Explain what event is foreshadowed by each example.

FORESHADOWING	LATER EVENT
Chapter 3 "That's what he [Cloyd] liked to do back in the canyon country: follow ledges across cliffs. You never knew what you might find."	
Chapter 5 Walter says, "She was scared to death of mines, thinkin' they're cavin' in all the time."	
Chapter 5 "Someday, he [Cloyd] vowed, he'd see those peaks up close. He would see the home of the Utes."	
Chapter 14 Walter says, "Drillin's hard work—can be dangerous, too."	
Chapter 15 Walter says, "Stay off of those peaks when the weather's comin' on. You know what that's about."	

Study Guide **37**

Glossary

Bearstone

- Words are listed by chapter in their order of appearance.
- The definition and the part of speech are based on the way the word is used in the chapter. For other uses of the word, check a dictionary.
- **Vocabulary Words** are preceded by an asterisk (*) and appear in the **Vocabulary Worksheet.**

Chapter 2

***foliage** *n.:* the leaves on a tree or bush

***intent** *adj.:* deeply interested; engrossed

***lush** *adj.:* luxuriant; full and rich

***impish** *adj.:* playful

insight *n.:* realization; understanding

Chapter 3

***gingerly** *adv.:* carefully

***swoon** *n.:* temporary loss of consciousness; a faint

precipice *n.:* steep or overhanging place

***exerted** *v.:* put forth

Chapter 4

admonish *v.:* scold

***devoid** *adj.:* empty; lacking

***dourly** *adv.:* sourly

potsherds *n.:* pieces of pottery

Chapter 5

***meager** *adj.:* scanty; empty

***skittish** *adj.:* easily frightened; jumpy

gait *n.:* manner of walking

Chapter 6

outfitter *n.:* hunting guide

Chapter 7

***scorching** *adj.:* very hot

beamed *v.:* smiled broadly

***tediously** *adv.:* tiresomely

Chapter 8

***mocking** *adj.:* ridiculing; insulting

Chapter 9

***stout** *adj.:* sturdy

***veered** *v.:* turned

thriving *adj.:* growing successfully

Chapter 10

***livid** *adj.:* purple with anger

revelation *n.:* discovery

Chapter 11

***adamant** *adj.:* firm; fixed

fluke *n.:* accidental or lucky event

Chapter 12

claustrophobic *adj.:* fearful of being trapped in a confined place

***conjectured** *v.:* guessed

Chapter 13

***swivel** *v.:* turn

coursed *v.:* flowed in a rush

Chapter 14

***reverie** *n.:* dreamlike state

vacantly *adv.:* without thought or emotion

Chapter 16

seared *v.:* burned

Chapter 17

***squelched** *v.:* crushed

Chapter 19

uncanny *adj.:* surprising and mysterious

***livelihood** *n.:* work; way of making a living

Chapter 20

***misgivings** *n.:* fears

verified *v.:* proven true

Chapter 22

***lounge** *n.:* a room for relaxing

Name _____ Date _____

Vocabulary Worksheet

Bearstone

A. Match each word in the two left-hand columns with the correct meaning from the two right-hand columns. Write the letter of the definition in the space provided.

WORD   DEFINITION

____ 1. meager   ____ 9. adamant   a. fears   h. tiresomely
____ 2. tediously   ____ 10. lush   b. insulting   i. guessed
____ 3. scorching   ____ 11. misgivings   c. room for relaxing   j. carefully
____ 4. conjectured   ____ 12. stout   d. scanty   k. purple with anger
____ 5. livid   ____ 13. exerted   e. put forth   l. firm; fixed
____ 6. veered   ____ 14. mocking   energetically   m. sturdy
____ 7. swoon   ____ 15. gingerly   f. very hot   n. a faint
____ 8. lounge   g. luxuriant   o. turned

B. *Synonyms* are words that are the same (or nearly the same) in meaning. Choose the synonym for each word in dark type. Write the letter of that synonym in the space provided.

____ 16. **intent:**
   a. engrossed   c. generous
   b. detached   d. sleeping

____ 17. **dourly:**
   a. sadly   c. sourly
   b. sweetly   d. deadly

____ 18. **foliage:**
   a. wrapping   c. envelope
   b. trickery   d. leaves

____ 19. **livelihood:**
   a. energetic   c. home
   b. joy   d. work

____ 20. **devoid:**
   a. nasty   c. despair
   b. empty   d. full

____ 21. **reverie:**
   a. daydream   c. forgetful
   b. denial   d. powerful

____ 22. **impish:**
   a. dangerous   c. playful
   b. skimpy   d. contented

____ 23. **swivel:**
   a. lie   c. sniffle
   b. turn   d. conquer

____ 24. **skittish:**
   a. jumpy   c. slippery
   b. scampering   d. careful

____ 25. **squelched:**
   a. squealed   c. crushed
   b. opened   d. echoed

Study Guide | 39

Name _____ Date _____

TEST — PART I: OBJECTIVE QUESTIONS

In the spaces provided, mark each true statement *T* and each false statement *F*. (20 points)

_____ 1. Leeno Atcitty, Cloyd's father, is in the hospital, recovering from a serious car accident.

_____ 2. Cloyd's housemother hopes that Walter Landis can help Cloyd do better in school.

_____ 3. The day he arrives at Walter's house, Cloyd adopts the secret name "Lone Bear."

_____ 4. The "Ancient Ones" are Walter's ancestors.

_____ 5. Walter's wife always said that a farm was a home.

_____ 6. In anger, Cloyd shoots the bear that has wandered through his carefully made fence.

_____ 7. Walter drives Cloyd to the group home and leaves him there after Cloyd refuses to help bale the hay.

_____ 8. Walter decides to reopen his mine, The Pride of the West.

_____ 9. Rusty lies about killing a grizzly bear to avoid losing his hunting license.

_____ 10. Cloyd saves Walter from freezing to death in a hailstorm.

Complete each sentence with the correct word or phrase from the box. (You will not use every item in the box.) (10 points)

sleep	read	horses	mummy
hamburgers	carved bear	peach trees	paintings
book	Lightning	Blueboy	frybread

11. Walter is especially proud of his deceased wife's beautiful _____.

12. In a cave, Cloyd finds a _____ and takes it as his special talisman.

13. Walter gives Cloyd a very precious gift, a horse that Cloyd names _____.

14. A food Cloyd really enjoys is _____.

15. Cloyd did not learn to _____ at the group home.

40 | Bearstone

Name _____ Date _____

TEST — PART II: SHORT-ANSWER QUESTIONS

Answer each question, using the lines provided. *(40 points)*

16. In the beginning of the novel, why does Cloyd go to visit his father?

17. Why did Walter give up mining many years ago?

18. What reasons does Cloyd have for working so hard for Walter?

19. Why does Cloyd want to climb to the top of the Rio Grande Pyramid?

20. How does Cloyd feel about Rusty? Why does he feel this way?

Study Guide | **41**

Name _____ Date _____

TEST — PART II: SHORT-ANSWER QUESTIONS *(continued)*

21. Walter decides to crush Cloyd's bearstone. What stops him from doing so?

22. Why does Cloyd return to Walter's house after Walter drove him back to his grandmother's home on the reservation?

23. Who are the "Weminuche," and what is Cloyd's connection to them?

24. Near the end of the novel, why does Cloyd frantically ride his horse in search of Rusty?

25. What does Cloyd buy for Walter at the very end of the story? Why?

Name _____ Date _____

TEST — PART III: ESSAY QUESTIONS

Choose *two* of the following topics. Use your own paper to write two or three paragraphs about each topic you choose. (*30 points*)

1. Cloyd believes that he is an unlucky person. Do you think that people make their own luck, or are they doomed to follow a specific path for life? Give examples from the novel to support your opinion.

2. Walter tells Cloyd that "the hurt you get over makes you stronger." Use examples from the novel to show how this statement is true or how it is not true.

3. It is obvious that Walter does a great deal for Cloyd. Describe how Cloyd helps Walter. Be specific.

4. Why is the bearstone so important to Cloyd? What does it represent to him? In which events in the novel does it play an important role?

5. At the end of the novel, Cloyd learns to live in what his grandmother calls a "good way." What does it mean to live in a "good way"? What characters live in a good way in the novel? Explain. How might people try to accomplish this goal in their lives?

_____

Use this space to make notes.

Study Guide | 43

Notes

Answer Key — Bearstone

Chapters 1–8: Making Meanings

READING CHECK

a. The authorities are afraid that his grandmother will not make him obey, and that she will let him run wild in the canyons again.

b. Walter's wife, now deceased, planted the trees. He cherishes them in her memory.

c. He finds a small piece of turquoise stone carved into the shape of a bear and the mummified remains of a baby.

d. He calls himself "Lone Bear."

1. Answers will vary. Students may say they admire his affection for the land. They may suggest that friendship with such a headstrong, embittered teenager would be challenging but not impossible. Encourage students to explain their responses.

2. Cloyd wants to get in touch with his heritage and his identity. Perhaps he also thinks that his father will take care of him, so that he does not have to return to the group home.

3. Possible responses include Walter's wife, love, growth, or creating a home in the wilderness.

4. Cloyd replaces the mummified infant where he found it and talks respectfully to the Ancient One, the spirit of the infant, about taking the bearstone.

5. Students may point out that Cloyd is alone, like a lone bear. In addition, bears represent good luck and strength to Utes, and Cloyd surely could use some good fortune in his life.

6. Rusty is a hunter and trapper; according to Walter, he is "the best outfitter in the San Juans." Cloyd does not like Rusty because he feels that the trapper mocks him.

7. Answers will vary. Students may refer to doing well on a test, winning a sporting event, or performing in a concert. Students may feel that they, like Cloyd, wanted to succeed to earn someone's approval, or their wishes may have been based more on personal goals.

8. Students probably will agree that love, kindness, consideration, and caring transform a house into a home.

9. Answers will vary. Students may say that *Bearstone* refers to strength and luck, and that the stone connects Cloyd to his Ute heritage. The title is fitting because the bearstone is the central symbol in the book, closely linked with the central character, Cloyd. Students might suggest other titles such as *Lone Bear, On My Own,* or *Cloyd's Life.*

Chapters 9–15: Making Meanings

READING CHECK

a. He wanted the trees to die slowly. "Before they died," Hobbs says, "their leaves would yellow and the peaches shrivel, and they would look just like his grandmother's peaches."

b. She wants to know if Walter "lives in a good way."

c. They stop at the graveyard to pay their respects to Walter's deceased wife.

d. Walter pretends that they are wasting their time at the mine—that there is no gold at all.

1. Answers will vary. Students may be put off by the strength of his anger but also may sympathize with his sense of loss over the damage that Cloyd has caused. In the chapters that follow, most students will come to appreciate Walter for his compassion and his attempts to help Cloyd, despite his disappointment.

2. Answers may vary. Students may say that Walter realizes that taking revenge on Cloyd won't accomplish anything. Smashing the bearstone won't restore the peach trees. They may say that

(cont.)

Answer Key (continued)

Bearstone

Walter doesn't want to hurt Cloyd the way that Cloyd has hurt him.

3. Cloyd realizes that Walter is a decent, kind person who "lives in a good way." Cloyd understands that Walter cares for him; indeed, Walter has become a surrogate father to Cloyd.

4. Cloyd shares these things because he feels a growing closeness to Walter.

5. For the first time, Cloyd realizes that a stranger could be concerned about his survival. This is a turning point in his life, the point at which he begins to emerge from his stony isolation.

6. The Rio Grande Pyramid represents the heart of the mountains to Cloyd. He feels it is a peak the Utes before him must have climbed. It thus represents his heritage.

7. Although students may understand that the climb was important to Cloyd, they may differ in their feelings about whether or not Walter should have let him do it and whether or not they would undertake such a journey.

8. Some students may hope that Walter will find gold because they want his determination to pay off. Other students might argue that if the mine contained gold, other prospectors would have found it already.

9. Answers may vary, but students may feel that specific words add to the novel's overall effectiveness because they make the descriptions much more precise and easier to visualize. Other students may feel that the words hinder their comprehension of a sentence.

Chapters 16–22: Making Meanings

READING CHECK

a. Blueboy is trapped in mud. Rather than kick free and risk crushing Cloyd's skull, Blueboy chooses to fall down the mountain and possibly injure or kill himself.

b. Cloyd rejoices in his union with nature and then performs an ancient Ute ceremony. He offers the bearstone to each of the Four Directions and then to the Earth and the Sky.

c. Rusty discovers that he has killed a grizzly bear. Since the grizzly is an endangered species, Rusty has committed a crime in killing it.

d. Cloyd replaces all the peach trees that he destroyed.

1. Most students will agree with Cloyd's decision to live with Walter because the boy and the man care deeply for each other.

2. There seems to be real affection between the horse and the boy. Earlier in the novel, Cloyd felt that the horse loved him, but Walter doubted that a horse was capable of love.

3. Cloyd no longer has the need to seek revenge on Rusty. Cloyd feels that Rusty's fear and guilt are punishment enough.

4. Cloyd wants to show how much he loves Walter and how grateful he is to him.

5.. Students may suggest that Walter nurtures Cloyd as a father nurtures a son—feeding him, teaching him, and loving him.

6. The crack may represent the "breakage" in Walter's life caused by his wife's death or it may represent the destroyed peach trees. Cloyd is the one who helps make Walter's life whole again.

7. Answers will vary, but most students will agree that it is important to have people who care about you and to care about them in return.

8. Answers will vary and may include movies and television shows as well as printed stories.

(cont.)

Answer Key (continued) — Bearstone

Encourage students to give specific examples in their comparisons. Examples may include *The Pigman* and "The Medicine Bag." Students may say that in these works, the young people and the older people learn from each other, come to trust each other, or come to love each other.

9. Other examples of foreshadowing include Cloyd's climb at the end of Chapter 2, Walter's mention of his late wife's fear of mines in Chapter 5, and Walter's talk of the dangers of drilling at the end of Chapter 14. In each case, the foreshadowing increases the suspense by raising questions in the reader's mind about what will happen.

Denning with the Great Bear
Making Meanings

> **READING CHECK**
> a. Hobbs started writing *Bearstone* when he got the surprising news that a grizzly bear had been killed in the San Juan Mountains, not far from where he and his wife were living.
> b. Hobbs got the idea for *Beardance* when a rancher spotted a mother grizzly bear and three cubs (suggesting that grizzly bears were not extinct in Colorado).

1. Students may point out that they learned about the inspiration for *Bearstone* and more about Hobbs's strong link to nature.

2. The title suggests that Hobbs has learned so much about bears that he feels like he is living ("denning") with them. In *Bearstone,* Cloyd feels a similar tie to bears.

3. Students may suggest that all people (whether they realize it or not) long for unspoiled nature.

4. Answers will be personal and need not be shared. Students might consider the inspirational power of nature or of a strong emotional experience, for example.

the earth is a living thing / Baby Bear Moon / Here on This Mountain
Making Meanings

> **READING CHECK**
> a. It is compared to a black bear.
> b. The speaker urges the listener not to bother bears and their cubs.
> c. They are some of the people, places, and things to which the speaker is linked. The speaker says, "I am" about them all.

1. Answers will vary but may include the following examples:
   - … it holds many animals and people all at once.
   - … leave it in peace.
   - … proud, as if anything were possible.

2. Clifton shows a variety of animals in vivid action—a shambling bear, a circling hawk—and refers to the minerals of the earth by speaking of diamonds. The earth itself is a "favorite child" of the universe.

3. Like the small child, Cloyd is lost in some ways. He runs away from the group home; he feels pain because of being abandoned by his father and by finding him comatose; and he is having trouble finding how he fits in the world. Also like the child, he feels a strong tie to bears.

4. Both have climbed a mountain; both feel connected with their American Indian heritage and with all of nature as they stand on the mountain.

5. All show a strong link to nature, an important relationship in *Bearstone.*

6. Most students probably will feel that it is highly unlikely that a human child could survive in the wilderness with wild animals because the child would not have the proper food, clothing, or shelter. Others may feel that a child could adapt to the wilderness, especially given the protection by a large animal.

Answer Key (continued)

Bearstone

Dancer: Making Meanings

> **READING CHECK**
> Events will vary but should include at least the following four: Clarissa arrives at her newest foster home; Clarissa goes to her first dance; Clarissa listens to music and learns to dance; and Clarissa joins the dancers at the story's end.

1. Students probably will feel joy at Clarissa's healing. The link between Clarissa and Molly Graybull isn't surprising because the child is looking for someone who can understand her and searching for a link to her heritage, and Molly represents both.

2. The narrator feels that Clarissa should be with them. She feels that Clarissa has already become part of the family. As such, the girl is treated with love and kindness.

3. As a link to her heritage, dancing gives Clarissa a sense of belonging and freedom.

4. She may symbolize acceptance, vitality, and heritage.

5. At first, both are filled with rage because of the neglect and mistreatment that they have suffered. By the end, however, both feel accepted and loved, have embraced their heritage, and have found something that is meaningful to them.

6. Students may suggest that using the foster mother as a narrator helps us see Clarissa's changes more distinctly than Clarissa herself might. Other students may suggest that the emotions in the story may be more intense, and therefore more interesting if Clarissa told it.

Lesson 1 / Lesson 2: Making Meanings

> **READING CHECK**
> a. A fierce thunderstorm passes through, leaving calm and a rainbow afterward.
> b. It takes place along the Rio Grande and in the desert.

1. Answers will vary. Sample responses follow.
   - …a woman who is afraid of a storm, but becomes calm after a storm passes.
   - …you can't stay sad forever. Or, …enjoy life.
   - …it takes place in the desert. Or, …the people find peace within themselves and hope for a better future.

2. Mora speaks of the desert's "face" and says that the desert "breathes deeply" and "smiles." Most of all, she compares it to a mother who whispers to her daughter ("Mi'ja") and urges her to work through her pain.

3. They are the sparkles of light where the sun strikes the river's surface, and they dance with the flow and chop of the water itself.

4. The poems paint a picture of the desert as an exciting, dramatic place, full of emotion and beauty.

My Friend Flicka: Making Meanings

> **READING CHECK**
> Events will vary but may be similar to these eight: Kennie begs for a colt; Mr. McLaughlin tells Kennie that he can choose a colt; Kennie chooses an "untamable" sorrel filly and names her "Flicka"; Flicka hurts herself badly when she runs into a wire fence; Kennie stays with her as she heals, but she will not let him near; she worsens, gets better, and then becomes deathly ill again; while helping Flicka, Kennie becomes deathly ill himself; and in time, both recover, and a bond is forged between them.

1. Some students will be surprised by the end of the story because it did not seem that Flicka would

(cont.)

48 | Bearstone

Answer Key (continued)   *Bearstone*

survive. Others will say the relationship between Kennie and Flicka is so powerful that they felt Flicka would live.

2. All three characters are misfits.

3. Mr. McLaughlin is motivated by his love for his wife and son. His action reveals his kindness and compassion.

4. Flicka's behavior suggests that animal and boy have an intuitive understanding and affection. This same relationship exists between Cloyd and Blueboy.

5. Answers will vary, but students may suggest that Kennie needs to prove his abilities and can do so by taking care of Flicka. Other students may suggest that Kennie needs to have something important to him, such as his relationship with Flicka, so that he can concentrate on school work.

6. Some students might say that they would do as Mr. McLaughlin has done, and order Flicka shot, because it appears that the animal will not survive. Other students, in contrast, would do everything in their power to save the horse because Kennie loves it.

The Name Game: Making Meanings

READING CHECK
a. If your name does not fit who you are as a person, the disharmony could cause illness.
b. Parents name their children according to the time of day and to the day of their birth, and according to any special circumstances surrounding the birth.
c. Tribal members blessed with visions inspired by the Creator were responsible for naming children.

1. Answers will vary. For example, some students may like the simplicity of names like *Ayo*. Others may prefer *Flying Hawk* because the translated name is linked to personal characteristics.

2. Names are important because they are powerful symbols that carry significant cultural meanings.

3. Students may suggest that the customs reveal the happiness people feel at the birth of a child and their attention to what was occurring at the time of the birth.

4. In choosing "Lone Bear," Cloyd selects a name linked to a personal characteristic, in keeping with the tradition of some American Indians.

5. Answers will be personal and need not be shared. Encourage students to think about what their new names would suggest to other people as well as to themselves.

Reading Skills and Strategies Worksheets

Chapters 1–8: Charting Causes and Effects
Answers may vary. Sample answers follow.

1. He is sent to live and work with rancher Walter Landis for the summer.

2. Walter misses her terribly.

3. He feels connected to his heritage and feels more confident.

4. He respects the mummified infant. He feels that bears should not be hunted. He has a strong tie to nature.

5. Cloyd experiences a new feeling of freedom. He develops a personal connection with the horse.

6. He wants to prove himself. He wants to show that he is not lazy.

7. Walter pays attention to Cloyd. Walter treats him with respect, cooks for him, gives him a horse, and takes him riding in the high country.

8. Cloyd admits to Walter that he cannot read.

9. Rusty treats Cloyd gruffly.

10. Cloyd is angry about Rusty's bear-hunting expedition. He senses that Rusty is Walter's true friend and that he, Cloyd, is not. He is angry with Walter.

Answer Key (continued)   *Bearstone*

Chapters 9–15: Completing a Story Triangle

Story triangles will vary. A sample triangle follows.

Cloyd Atcitty
strong quiet
southwest Colorado mountains
asking who he is
trying to honor his heritage
angry with people who hunt bear
wondering about his place in the world
works with people who love and respect him

Chapters 16–22: Using a Time Line

Events listed may vary. A sample listing follows.

1. Cloyd and Blueboy have an accident on their way to the Rio Grande Pyramid.
2. Cloyd reaches the mountaintop.
3. Rusty gets Cloyd to tell him about the bear Cloyd spotted in the mountains.
4. Cloyd witnesses Rusty's killing the grizzly while Walter has an accident checking his missed shots.
5. Cloyd rescues Walter.
6. Cloyd decides not to turn Rusty in.
7. Cloyd chooses to stay with Walter to help him recuperate.
8. Cloyd replaces Walter's peach trees.

Answers will vary. Some students may believe that Cloyd's decision not to turn Rusty in is the most important.

Literary Elements Worksheets

Figures of Speech

1. simile
2. simile
3. personification
4. simile
5. simile and personification
6. personification
7. metaphor
8. personification
9. simile
10. simile

Foreshadowing

Chapter 3 Cloyd finds the bearstone.

Chapter 5 The mine caves in on Walter.

Chapter 5 Cloyd sees the peaks up close. He ascends the Rio Grande Pyramid.

Chapter 14 Walter has a mining accident.

Chapter 15 Answers may vary. Students might suggest that since the good weather holds, the words foreshadow the moment when Cloyd and Blueboy have an accident; when Cloyd witnesses Rusty killing a grizzly; or when Walter has a mining accident.

Vocabulary Worksheet

If you wish to score this worksheet, assign the point values given in parentheses.

A. (4 points each)   **B.** (4 points each)

1. d	9. l	16. a	24. a
2. h	10. g	17. c	25. c
3. f	11. a	18. d	
4. i	12. m	19. d	
5. k	13. e	20. b	
6. o	14. b	21. a	
7. n	15. j	22. c	
8. c		23. b	

Test

Part I: Objective Questions

1. F
2. T
3. T
4. F
5. T
6. F
7. F
8. T
9. T
10. F
11. peach trees
12. carved bear
13. Blueboy
14. frybread
15. read

Answer Key (continued) — *Bearstone*

Part II: Short-Answer Questions

16. Cloyd is seeking his heritage, ties to his family, and roots. He hopes that his father will be able to supply these answers, but he finds that his father is unable to help him in any way.

17. His wife was afraid that he would get badly injured or even killed in a mining accident.

18. Cloyd is trying to prove that the old man was right to trust him. He wants to prove that he can accomplish something of value.

19. At the top of the Pyramid, Cloyd feels that he is a part of it all, "like the beating heart of the mountains is your own heart." On the top of the mountain, he can get in touch with his heritage.

20. Cloyd hates and resents Rusty because he feels the trapper is laughing at him. He also resents Rusty's way of making a living—hunting.

21. Walter realizes that nothing would be accomplished by destroying the bearstone, that hurting Cloyd would not make Walter feel any better nor would it make up for damage Cloyd did to the trees.

22. Cloyd wants another chance to show Walter that he appreciates the man's efforts and that he is a valuable human being.

23. They are the ancient Utes who lived in the region. As such, they are Cloyd's ancestors.

24. Walter has been badly injured in a mining accident. Cloyd intercepts the helicopter that Rusty has called to pick up the dead grizzly bear. Because that helicopter takes Walter to the hospital, Cloyd has saved Walter's life.

25. Cloyd buys Walter peach trees to show his appreciation for everything Walter has done for him and to apologize for destroying Walter's previous trees. By replacing the trees he has destroyed, Cloyd is trying to create a new life with Walter.

Part III: Essay Questions

Students should respond to two out of the five essay questions. Answers will vary, but most should include specific references to the text.

1. Some students may argue that Cloyd is indeed unlucky, as shown by his mother's death, his father's terminal condition, and his great poverty. His bad luck continues in his failure in school and inability to flourish in the group home. Other students, in contrast, may argue that Cloyd experiences great good fortune when he meets Walter and matures sufficiently to appreciate Walter's love.

2. Students may say that Cloyd becomes stronger after his anguish at seeing the body of the bear that one of Rusty's clients has killed. He is able to put aside vengeful feelings toward Rusty when Rusty later kills a grizzly. He is also upset by the hurt he has caused Walter by killing Walter's trees. Cloyd realizes what a strong relationship they have and works to restore Walter's confidence and trust in him. Walter gets over the hurt of losing his wife by developing a close relationship with Cloyd and by helping Cloyd find his way.

3. On the most obvious level, Cloyd saves Walter's life in the mining accident. On a less obvious level, Cloyd helps Walter recover from the despair that he felt following his wife's death.

4. The bearstone is important to Cloyd because it provides a link to his heritage and culture. It helps him find his identity. Events should include Cloyd's finding the buried infant, Walter's threatening to smash the stone, Cloyd's giving the stone to Walter.

Study Guide | 51

Answer Key (continued)

Bearstone

5. Students may suggest that following the Golden Rule is an excellent way to lead a "good life"—a life filled with kindness, respect for others, and social usefulness. Students may say that Cloyd learns to live in a good way by helping Walter; that Walter lives in a good way as shown by his love for his wife, by the care that he takes of the farm because of her, and through the love he shows Cloyd; and that Cloyd's grandmother lives in a good way because she honors her heritage. Students also may suggest that the best way to accomplish this goal is to get busy and do kind and useful things for others rather than just make plans to live better.

Notes

Notes